W9-ASF-007

3 1865 00135 9990

J
746.43
SAD

SADLER, Judy Ann
Knitting

WITHDRAWN

1106, 15x, 11/05 LC

RIVER FOREST PUBLIC LIBRARY
735 Lathrop Avenue
River Forest, Illinois 60305
708 / 366-5205

Knitting

Written by Judy Ann Sadler
Illustrated by Esperança Melo

KIDS CAN PRESS

To the wondrous women who helped me knit this book together:
my sister-in-law Deb Sadler, my mom Rieka Bertens,
my mom-in-law Barb Sadler and my editor Laurie Wark.

Text © 2002 Judy Ann Sadler
Illustrations © 2002 Esperança Melo

KIDS CAN DO IT and the 📕 logo are trademarks of Kids Can Press Ltd.

All rights reserved. No part of this publication may be reproduced, stored in a retrieval
system or transmitted, in any form or by any means, without the prior written
permission of Kids Can Press Ltd. or, in case of photocopying or other reprographic
copying, a license from CANCOPY (Canadian Copyright Licensing Agency),
1 Yonge Street, Suite 1900, Toronto, ON, M5E 1E5.

Many of the designations used by manufacturers and sellers to distinguish their products are
claimed as trademarks. Where those designations appear in this book and Kids Can Press Ltd. was
aware of a trademark claim, the designations have been printed in initial capital letters (e.g., Velcro).

Neither the Publisher nor the Author shall be liable for any damage, which
may be caused or sustained as a result of conducting any of the activities in this
book without specifically following instructions, conducting the activities without
proper supervision, or ignoring the cautions contained in the book.

Kids Can Press acknowledges the financial support of the Government of Canada,
through the BPIDP, for our publishing activity.

Published in Canada by   Published in the U.S. by
Kids Can Press Ltd.   Kids Can Press Ltd.
29 Birch Avenue   2250 Military Road
Toronto, ON M4V 1E2   Tonawanda, NY 14150

www.kidscanpress.com

Edited by Laurie Wark
Designed by Karen Powers
Photography by Frank Baldassarra
Printed in Hong Kong, China, by Wing King Tong Company Limited

The hardcover edition of this book is smyth sewn casebound.
The paperback edition of this book is limp sewn with a drawn-on cover.

CM 02 0 9 8 7 6 5 4 3 2 1
CM PA 02 0 9 8 7 6 5 4 3 2 1

National Library of Canada Cataloguing in Publication Data

Sadler, Judy Ann, 1959–
Knitting

(Kids can do it)

ISBN 1-55337-050-3 (bound)   ISBN 1-55337-051-1 (pbk.)

1. Knitting. I. Melo, Esperança. II. Title. III. Series.

TT820.S22 2001   746.43'2   C2001-903316-8

Kids Can Press is a **Corus**™ Entertainment Company

Contents

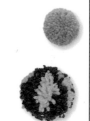

Getting started

It's like magic to be able to turn yarn into great knitted items that you can wear or give as special gifts. You can knit a fun tasseled hat and book bag for yourself, slipper socks for your brother and a mini-purse for your friend. How about knitting Grandma a cozy ribbed scarf or your aunt a funky boa? You can knit when you're with your friends, watching TV or talking on the phone, and you can take your knitting wherever you go. When you know how to cast on, knit and purl, the whole world of knitting is yours to discover. And there's always something new — gorgeous yarns, cool colors and great ideas to try. So begin with a scarf and have fun making the projects in this book. Once you get tangled up with yarn, you'll have a ball.
Happy knitting!

MATERIALS

Yarn

There are so many different types of yarn that you're sure to find some you like. The most common yarns are wool (made from the fleece of sheep), cotton and synthetics such as acrylic and polyester. Yarns often have a mixture of fibers in them. The weight (thickness) of a yarn is marked on the label. If you need a certain weight of yarn for a project in this book, it will be in the list of things you need. Fabulous new colors and types of yarn are always becoming available. Try feathery light or thick soft acrylics, sparkling blends, playful chenille or fine, washable merino wool.

Knitting needles

The needles you need for the projects in this book are straight and have a knob at one end so that your stitches can't fall off. Needles are sized in millimeters and by American standard numbers. They come in different lengths, too. The most common are 25 cm and 35 cm (10 in. and 14 in.) long. You may find it most comfortable to use 25 cm (10 in.) needles, as the longer ones often get caught on your sleeves or chair.

Needle gauge

A needle gauge is a knitting ruler with holes in it. Use it to figure out what size your needles are in case they are not marked in both millimeters and American sizes.

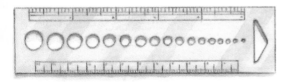

Point protectors or stoppers

Use these small rubber caps on the tips of your needles when you aren't knitting. They keep the stitches on the needles and prevent the needles from poking through your knitting bag. If you don't have any, wind a rubber band around the tip of each needle.

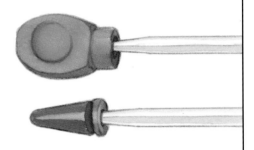

Yarn needle

Yarn needles are also called craft, plastic canvas or knitters needles. They have a blunt tip and large eye.

Scissors

Use scissors that have short blades sharp enough to easily cut yarn.

Stitch holders

These holders are handy to have, but can often be substituted with large safety pins.

Yarn tips
and tails

WINDING YARN

Yarn often comes in a ball that is ready to use. If it comes in a skein, wind the yarn into a ball before using it, to avoid tangles. Remove the label and untwist the skein. Cut off any yarn tied around the skein to hold it together. Loop the bundle of yarn around the back of a chair or someone's hands. Take one yarn end and wind it around two fingers about five times. Slide the yarn off your fingers and start loosely winding the yarn into a ball. As you wind, turn the ball to make an even shape. When you are finished, tuck the end under a couple of strands of yarn, where you can easily get hold of it when you are ready to knit.

FINDING THE YARN END

With a store-bought ball of yarn, it is best to pull the yarn end out from the center of the ball. If you pull out a clump of yarn along with the end, that's okay. You will use it up as you knit.

AVOIDING TANGLES

To keep yarn clean and free of tangles, put the ball into a small, clear plastic bag. Pull the yarn end out. Use a twist tie or piece of yarn to tie the bag closed. You should be able to pull the yarn freely from the bag as you knit.

KEEPING RECORDS

Keep your yarn labels because they list important information such as the fiber content, washing instructions and dye lot of the yarn. The dye lot is a number given by the manufacturer for the color of the yarn. If you run out of yarn, try to get more from the same dye lot so that it will match the yarn you've been using. Since the store may run out, it is best to buy a little extra yarn at the beginning of the project. If you don't use it, most stores will let you return a new ball of yarn. Or add it to your yarn collection, so you always have some when you are ready to knit again.

KEEPING NOTES

It's fun to keep a knitting notebook or scrapbook. Tape or staple a small piece of yarn, its label, and a description or photograph of what you made with the yarn into a notebook. You will enjoy going through your notebook in years to come.

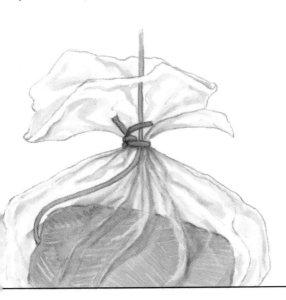

Casting on

Casting on means to put on the first row of stitches. Refer to these pages whenever the instructions say to cast on.

1 Make a slip knot in the yarn, as shown.

2 Pick up a needle in your right hand and rest your index finger along the needle. Put the slip knot on this needle so that the short end of the yarn is closest to you. Pull on the yarn ends so that the slip knot fits loosely on the needle.

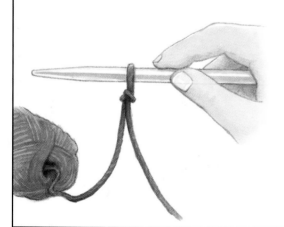

3 Put your left thumb and index finger between the two strands of yarn hanging down. Grasp both strands with the other three fingers on your left hand.

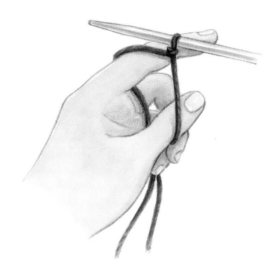

4 Spread apart your index finger and thumb. Turn your left hand so that your palm is toward you.

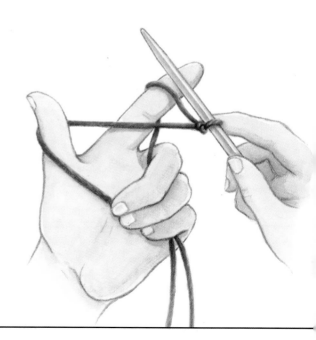

5 Keep the yarn tight as you dip the tip of the needle toward you, then up into the loop on your thumb.

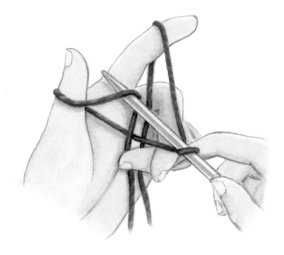

7 Direct the tip of the needle down into the center of the loop on your thumb, and bring it out under the strand of yarn closest to you. Point the tip of the needle upward.

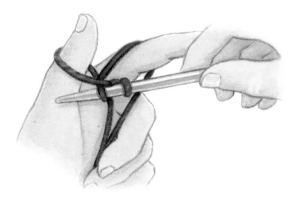

6 Turn your left hand so that your palm is sideways to you. Direct the tip of the needle toward your index finger and down into the center of the loop there to pick it up. Point the needle upward and turn your palm back toward you.

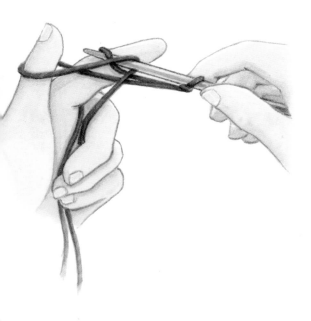

8 Allow the loop to slide off your thumb. Gently pull down on the strand and up with the needle to tighten the new stitch onto the needle. It should be closer to the tip of the needle than the slip knot is.

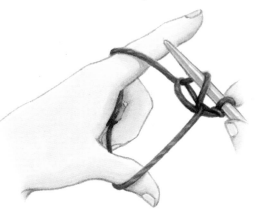

9 Repeat from step 4 until you have cast on all the stitches you need.

Knit stitch

To begin the knit stitch, you need a pair of knitting needles with stitches cast on one of them (page 8).

1 Hold the needle with the stitches on it in your left hand.

2 Take the empty needle in your right hand. Slide the tip up into the first stitch and push it behind the left needle, to form an **X**.

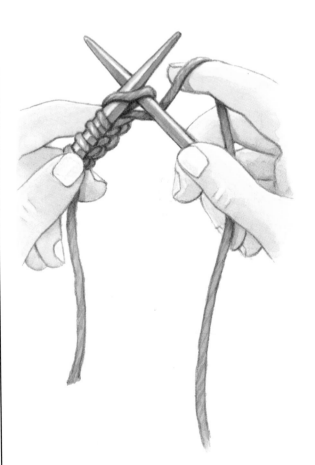

3 With your right hand, wind the working yarn (coming from the ball) behind and around the right needle in a counter-clockwise direction. The yarn should go between the needles.

4 Dip the needle down and toward you so that it goes under and through the stitch on the left needle. The right needle should be in front of the left one and have one loop of yarn on it.

5 Slide the right needle upward so that the stitch comes off the left needle and stays on the right one. You have completed one knit stitch. Finish the row by repeating steps 1 to 5, then move the full needle to your left hand and begin row 2.

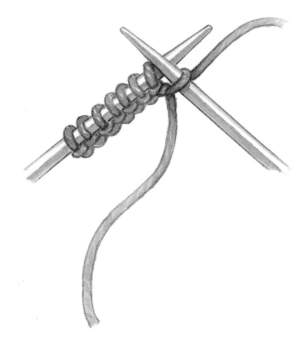

A NOTE FOR LEFTIES

Since both your hands will be busy as you knit, you may find that even if you are left-handed you will be able to knit right-handed. However, if you like, you can reverse the instructions by changing "right" to "left" and "left" to "right."

A FEW TIPS

• The first stitch is the most difficult to knit because it sometimes gets big and loose. Keep it small by firmly holding on to the working yarn.

• Don't get discouraged if the first few rows aren't perfect. Begin one of the projects, and you'll soon find your own knitting style.

• Before you put your knitting down, finish the row you are knitting. This saves confusion when you pick up your needles the next time.

• If you get a chance, watch someone who knits often to see how he or she does it. Some knitters tuck one needle under their arm. Some position their right hand so they can loop the yarn over the needle with their index finger. Others knit so quickly you can hardly see what they're doing!

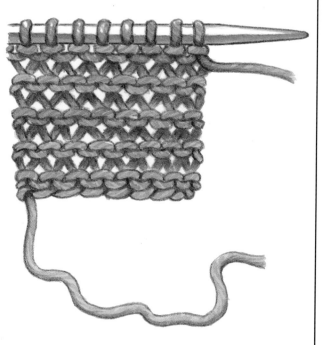

Purl stitch

Once you are comfortable with the knit stitch (page 10), the purl stitch is easy to do. To begin the purl stitch, you need a pair of knitting needles with stitches cast on one of them (page 8).

1 Hold the needle with the stitches on it in your left hand and the empty needle in your right hand.

2 With the working yarn in the front, slide the empty needle down into the first stitch so that the right needle is in front of the left needle.

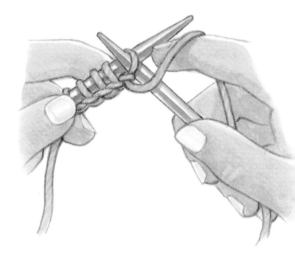

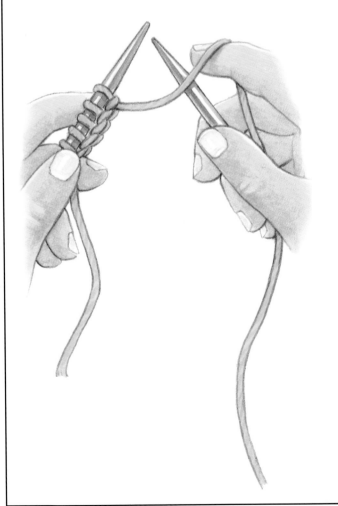

3 Use your right hand to wrap the working yarn around the right needle in a counter-clockwise direction.

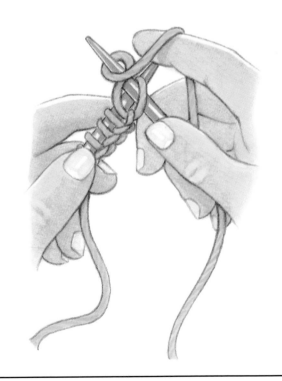

4 Hold the right needle and the yarn with your right hand. Don't let the yarn come off as you push the tip of this needle down through the stitch on the left needle. The right needle should be behind the left one and have one loop of yarn on it.

5 Lift up the right needle so that the stitch comes off the left needle and stays on the right one. You have completed one purl stitch.

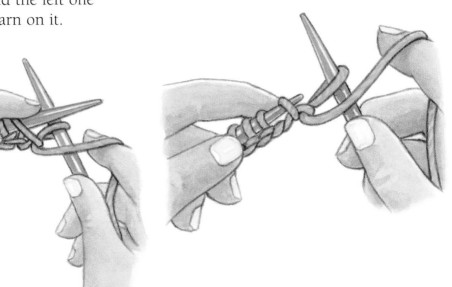

6 Finish the row by repeating steps 1 to 5, then move the full needle to your left hand and begin row 2.

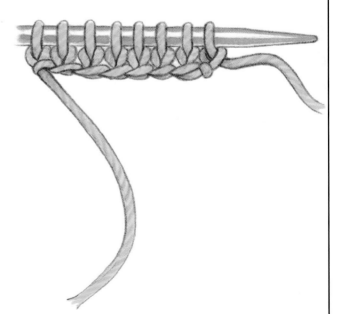

Increasing

For some projects, you will need to increase the number of stitches you are knitting to help shape your item. The instructions tell you when you should increase.

1 Begin a knit stitch as usual (page 10), by putting the right needle into a stitch on the left needle.

2 Knit the stitch, but just before you slide it off the left needle, put the right needle into the back of the stitch you just knit.

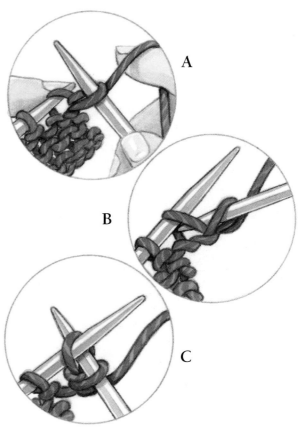

A

B

C

3 Knit the stitch again and slide the old stitch off the left needle. You will have an extra stitch on the right needle. You've made two stitches out of one.

Decreasing

Sometimes you will need to decrease the number of stitches you are knitting to help shape your item.

1 Instead of putting the tip of the right needle into one stitch on the left needle, put the right needle into two stitches.

2 Knit the stitches together as if they were one. They may feel a little tight. You will have one less stitch on the right needle.

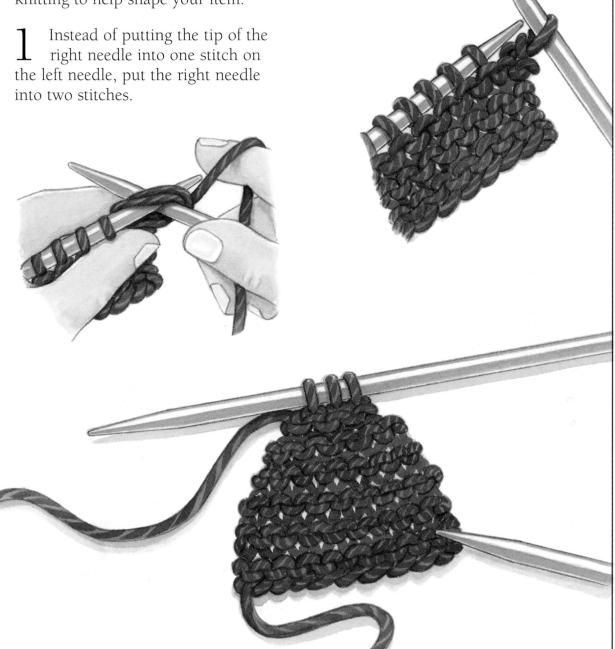

Casting off

Casting off is also known as binding off. This is how you take the last row of stitches off the needle so that your knitting does not unravel.

1 Knit the first two stitches onto the right needle as usual (page 10).

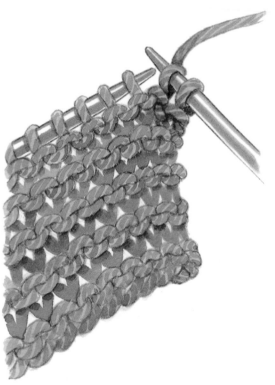

2 Use the left needle (or your fingers) to lift the first stitch (the one farthest from the tip) over the second one and off the end of the right needle.

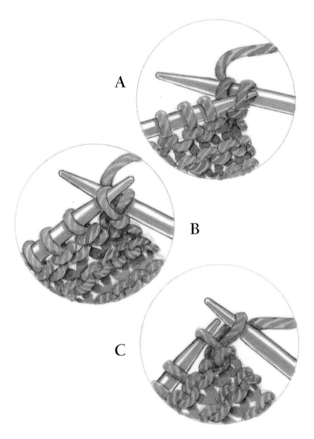

A

B

C

3 Knit the next stitch. Again, lift the first stitch over the second one and let it off. Continue until there are no stitches on the left needle and just one on the right needle.

4 Cut the yarn, leaving a 20 cm (8 in.) tail. Pull gently on the last stitch to make it larger. Remove the knitting needle. Bring the yarn tail through the loop and pull it snug.

6 If you are casting off when you have been knitting ribbing, you should cast off in the same knit and purl pattern.

5 Use a yarn needle to weave the yarn tail in and out of the knitting, then trim it off.

Pom-pom scarf

When you knit every row, this is called the garter stitch. By using thick, soft yarn and large knitting needles, you'll have a cozy scarf before you know it!

YOU WILL NEED

- a 100 g (3 ½ oz.) ball of chunky, bulky or thicker weight yarn
- knitting needles, size 9 to 12 mm (U.S. 13 to 17)
- yarn for pom-poms
- a ruler or measuring tape, scissors, a yarn needle

1 Make a slip knot 115 cm (45 in.) from the end of the yarn. Cast on (page 8) 20 loose stitches. (You can cast on 16 stitches if your yarn is very thick.)

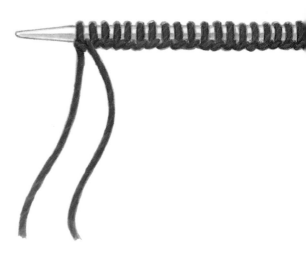

2 As you knit the first stitch (page 10), make sure you are using working yarn from the ball, not the leftover tail, to make the stitch.

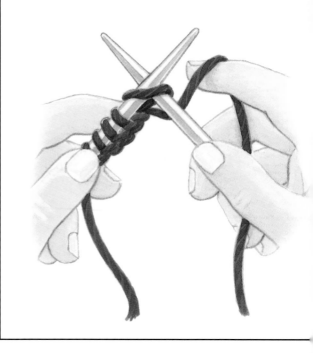

3 When you begin the second stitch, pull on the working yarn so that the first stitch is snug on the right needle. Knit the rest of the row.

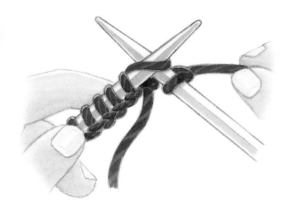

4 Move the needle with the stitches on it from your right to left hand and knit row 2.

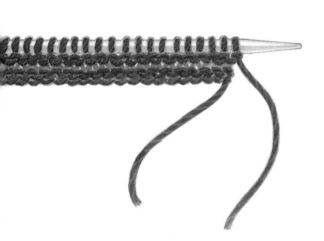

5 Keep knitting. When your scarf is about 1 m (1 yd.), or as long as you want it to be, cast off the stitches (page 16).

6 Use a yarn needle to weave in the two yarn tails.

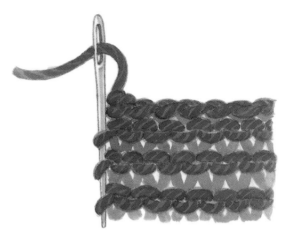

7 See page 38 to make four pom-poms. You can make them all the same color or each a different color. Use the tying yarn ends to knot a pom-pom to each corner of the scarf. Cut off the yarn ends.

OTHER IDEAS

Make a fringe (steps 6 and 7, page 25) for your scarf. Or put a tassel (page 39) on each corner.

Patterned headband

To make this headband, you will create a pattern using a combination of knit and purl stitches.

YOU WILL NEED

- a small ball of chunky weight yarn
- knitting needles, size 5.5 or 6 mm (U.S. 9 or 10)
- a ruler or measuring tape, a pencil and paper, scissors, a yarn needle

1 Make a slip knot 50 cm (20 in.) from the end of the yarn and cast on (page 8) 12 stitches.

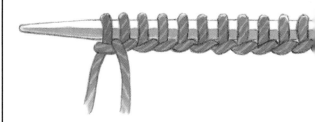

2 On a sheet of paper, write down the following pattern:

row 1: knit	**row 5:** knit
row 2: purl	**row 6:** knit
row 3: knit	**row 7:** knit
row 4: purl	**row 8:** knit

3 Knit (page 10) row 1 and check it off on the paper. Purl (page 12) row 2 and check it off. Continue through row 8, then begin at row 1 again. (You may want to check off the rows in a different color each time you go through the pattern.)

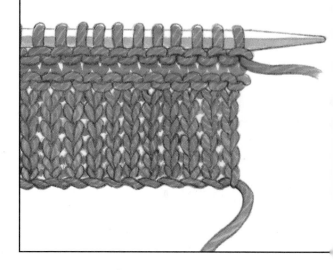

4 Continue until you have about 40 cm (16 in.). Hold the ends of the headband together and try it on. Make it longer if it doesn't fit.

5 Cast off (page 16), leaving a 60 cm (24 in.) tail.

6 Thread the tail into the yarn needle and stitch the ends together to form a circle. Make a couple of stitches in the same spot, weave the tail in and out of the knitting, and cut the yarn. Weave in the tail from the beginning of your knitting.

OTHER IDEAS

• To make a reversible headband, knit another headband in a different color. (You may want to keep it simple by knitting every row.) Place it inside the first one. Stitch the two headbands together around both outside edges.

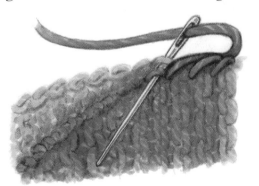

• Make a hair band by casting on 4 stitches and knitting 40 cm (16 in.).

Rolled-brim hat

This hat is made using a stocking (stockinette) stitch, which means that you knit one row and purl the next. Because this hat requires many stitches, use 35 cm (14 in.) knitting needles if you have them.

YOU WILL NEED

- 2 different-colored balls of chunky weight yarn
- knitting needles, size 5 mm (U.S. 8)
- a ruler or measuring tape, scissors, a yarn needle

1 Using the color of yarn for the rolled brim, make a slip knot 2.5 m (2 ½ yds.) from the end of the yarn. Cast on 70 stitches.

2 To keep track of whether you should knit or purl a row, mark the knob end of the empty knitting needle with a piece of yarn or tape. Whenever the stitches are on the marked needle, it is time to purl.

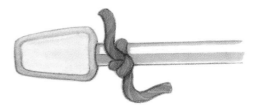

3 Knit row 1. Now the stitches are on the marked needle.

4 Purl row 2. Continue the knit and purl pattern until you have about 5 cm (2 in.) of the first color. The knitting will start to curl at the edge.

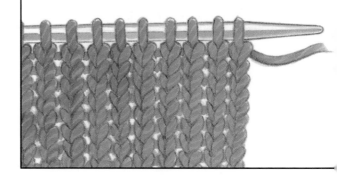

5 To change colors, make sure that you have just purled a row and that all the stitches are on the unmarked needle. Cut the working yarn, leaving a 15 cm (6 in.) tail. Knot the new color close to the edge of your knitting.

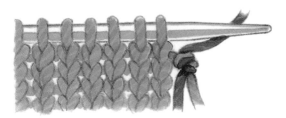

6 Begin knitting with the new color. Keep the knot at the edge, rather than pulling it through the first few stitches.

7 Continue the knit and purl pattern until you have about 18 cm (7 in.) of the second color. Cast off, leaving a 60 cm (24 in.) tail.

8 Thread the long tail into the yarn needle. Fold the hat in half with the good sides together and stitch as shown.

9 Thread more yarn into the needle and make a knot at the longer end. Arrange the hat so the new seam is down the center of the back. Uncurl the top and stitch it closed. Turn the hat right side out.

10 If you like, make two pompoms (page 38) or tassels (page 39) and stitch one to each corner.

Ribbed scarf

Knitting and purling stitches in each row creates ribbing. Stripes of color, wide ribbing and a thick fringe make this scarf as much fun to make as it is to wear.

YOU WILL NEED

- 3 or 4 different-colored balls of chunky or worsted weight yarn
- knitting needles, size 5 mm (U.S. 8)
- a 10 cm (4 in.) square of cardboard
- a ruler or measuring tape, scissors, a yarn needle

1 Make a slip knot about 150 cm (60 in.) from the end of one color of yarn. Cast 45 stitches onto an unmarked needle (step 2, page 22).

2 Knit the first 3 stitches. Bring the working yarn to the front and purl the next 3 stitches. Put the yarn to the back to knit the next 3 and so on. Knit 3 and purl 3 to the end of the row, ending with knitting 3. All the stitches should be on the marked needle.

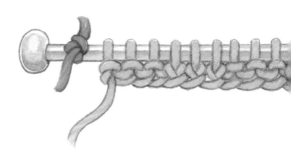

3 Begin row 2 by purling the first 3 stitches. Then knit 3 and purl 3 to the end of the row. You will see the ribbing beginning to form as you continue this pattern. When the stitches are on the marked needle, begin and end with 3 purl stitches.

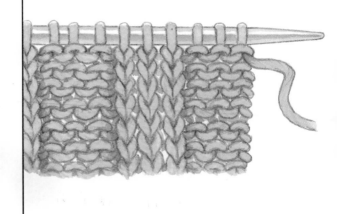

4 When you have about 6 cm (2 ¼ in.) and your stitches are on the unmarked needle, change the color of the yarn (steps 5 and 6, page 23).

5 Continue with the ribbing and color changes until your scarf is about 1 m (1 yd.) or as long as you want it to be. Use the knit and purl pattern when you cast off. Cut the yarn and weave in all the loose tails with the yarn needle.

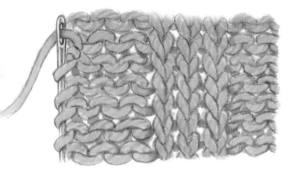

6 Choose one yarn color and wrap it around the cardboard about 60 times. Cut the yarn from the ball. Cut the yarn on the cardboard on one end only. Repeat to make 60 more pieces of yarn.

7 Fold 4 pieces of the yarn in half. Pull open a stitch along one end of the scarf. Push the loop end of the folded yarn into the stitch and pull the yarn ends through the loop. Finish the fringe on both ends of the scarf.

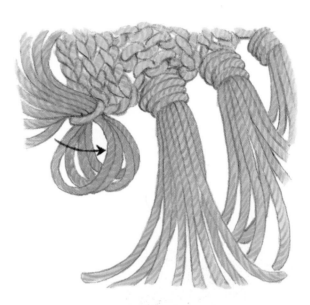

OTHER IDEAS

Use two or more colors of yarn for the fringe or make a pom-pom (page 38) fringe.

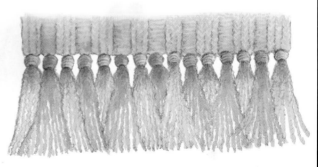

Slipper socks

You can decorate the sock bottoms with dimensional fabric paint so they are non-slip. To make larger socks, use chunky or bulky yarn and size 5.75 to 8 mm (U.S. 10 to 11) needles.

YOU WILL NEED

- 2 different-colored balls of double knit (DK) weight yarn, 50 g (1¾ oz.) each
- knitting needles, size 4.5 mm (U.S. 7)
- a ruler or measuring tape, scissors, a yarn needle

1 Make a slip knot about 120 cm (47 in.) from the end of one color of yarn. Cast 42 stitches onto an unmarked needle (step 2, page 22).

2 Knit the first 2 stitches. Bring the working yarn to the front and purl the next 2 stitches. Knit 2 and purl 2 to the end of the row, ending with knitting 2. All the stitches should be on the marked needle.

3 For row 2, purl 2 stitches, knit 2, purl 2 to the end of the row.

4 Repeat steps 2 and 3 twice so that you have knitted six rows and all the stitches are on the unmarked needle.

5 To change colors, do not cut the first color of yarn. Simply knot the new one to it as close to the knitting as you can.

6 Knit and purl for two rows of the second color. You should be back to the side where you tied the new color. Whenever you reach this edge, twist the two strands of color together, but keep knitting with the second color.

7 After six rows, change colors again. This time, simply pick up the first color, rather than tie it on. Knit until you have about 16 stripes, or more if you want longer socks.

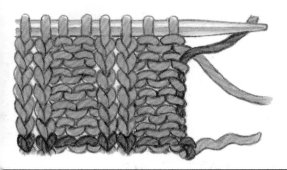

8 To finish, do not cast off. Cut one of the yarns, leaving a short tail, and cut the other, leaving a 120 cm (47 in.) tail. Knot the two colors of yarn together.

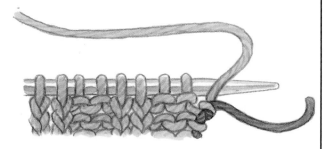

9 Thread the long tail into the yarn needle and use it to gather all the stitches off the knitting needle. Pull tightly so the stitches are in a tiny circle at the toe area. Make a couple of stitches in one spot to hold the gathered stitches, then stitch the long side seam all the way to the top. Knot your sewing yarn to the yarn end you find there, cut both and weave in the ends. Turn the sock right side out, to hide the seam. Make another sock.

Cozy blanket

Knit this blanket made up of many colorful squares, then make a pillow to match.

YOU WILL NEED

- chunky or bulky weight yarn in different colors
- knitting needles, size 6 or 7 mm (U.S. 10 or 10½)
- a ruler or measuring tape, scissors, a yarn needle

1 Make a slip knot about 70 cm (28 in.) from the end of one color of yarn and cast on 20 stitches.

2 Knit every stitch in every row until you have a square, about 40 rows. To know if your knitting is square, fold it diagonally. When it makes a triangle, it is square. Cast off and weave in the ends.

3 Knit 20 or more different-colored squares. Lay them out on the floor so you can decide how you'd like your blanket to look. Make a pattern of colors, place the squares randomly, or turn some sideways so that their knitting lines go opposite to those of the squares next to them.

4 If you want the stitches to stand out, use a contrasting yarn color to your blanket and make large stitches. Otherwise, choose one of the colors in the blanket and sew 2 squares together with small stitches. Add more squares until you finish the row.

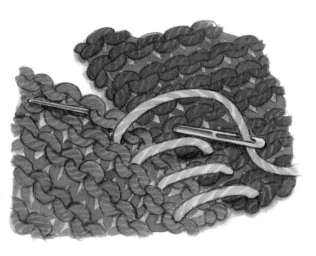

5 Sew the other squares into strips, then match the corners of the squares and stitch the strips together.

PILLOW

You will need the supplies from page 28 as well as polyester fiberfill stuffing or a pillow form to make this cozy cushion.

1 Cast on about 30 stitches and knit a square (step 2, page 28). Make a second square the same size, but in a different color.

2 Stitch the squares most of the way around.

3 Stuff with polyester fiberfill or a pillow form, and stitch the pillow closed.

4 To finish, make four pom-poms (page 38) or tassels (page 39) and stitch one to each corner, or add a fringe (steps 6 and 7, page 25) all around.

Book bag

This book bag is knitted with thin needles for small tight stitches. It takes longer to knit than most projects in this book, but the bag will be soft and strong.

YOU WILL NEED

- about 200 g (7 oz.) of Aran weight cotton yarn
- knitting needles, size 3.25 mm (U.S. 3)
- a button
- a needle and thread
- a ruler or measuring tape, scissors, a yarn needle

1 Make a slip knot about 1.5 m (1 ½ yd.) from the end of the yarn. Cast on 65 stitches.

2 Knit every row until you have about 45 cm (18 in.) of garter stitch. Cast off the stitches.

3 Fold the knitting in half and stitch the side seams closed. Turn the bag right side out.

4 To make the strap, cast on 12 stitches. (If you wish, use size 4.5 mm [U.S. 7] needles.) Knit every row until the strap is about 90 cm (36 in.) or as long as you want it to be. Stitch the strap to the inside top of the side seams of the bag.

5 Finger crochet (see below) a loop for your book bag closure, and stitch it to the center top edge. Sew a button on the opposite side.

FINGER CROCHET

This crochet cord is great for closures and straps, but you can also use it for a ponytail holder, hair band, shoelaces or decorative garland.

1 Make a slip knot about 15 cm (6 in.) from the end of the working yarn.

2 Pull a new loop of yarn through from behind the slip-knot loop and tighten the slip-knot loop.

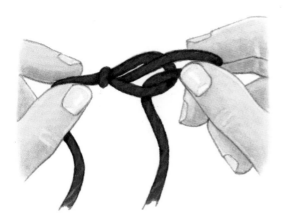

3 Continue pulling a new loop of yarn through the existing one. Keep the stitches fairly loose.

4 When you have as much crocheting as you need, cut the yarn, bring the end through the loop, and pull it tight.

Mini-purse

This purse is perfect for some money, lip balm and a key, and it won't take long to make!

YOU WILL NEED

- a small ball of knitting worsted weight yarn
- knitting needles, size 4.5 mm (U.S. 7)
- a button
- a needle and thread
- a ruler or measuring tape, scissors, a yarn needle

1 Make a slip knot about 75 cm (30 in.) from the end of the yarn and cast 18 stitches onto an unmarked needle (step 2, page 22).

2 Do not trim the long tail. Knit every row until you have about 20 cm (8 in.) of garter stitch and all the stitches are on the unmarked needle.

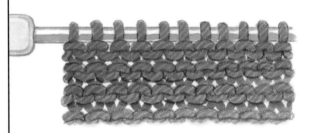

3 To make the flap, begin to decrease (page 15). Knit the first 2 stitches together and knit the last 2 stitches together in this row.

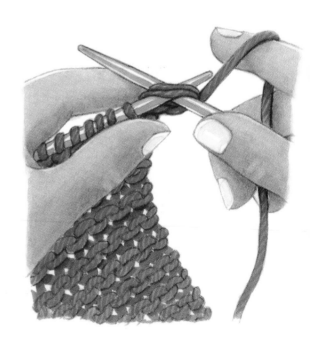

4 Knit all the stitches in the next row, then decrease at the beginning and end of the next row. Keep decreasing by 2 stitches every time the stitches are on the unmarked needle, until there are 2 stitches left.

5 To make the button loop, knit the 2 remaining stitches until the piece is about 4 cm (1 ½ in.) long.

6 Cast off and cut the yarn, leaving a 20 cm (8 in.) tail. Thread it into the yarn needle and fasten the end of your knitting into a loop.

7 Sew the side seams with the yarn tail from step 1. Weave in the end and turn the purse right side out.

8 Sew the button in place.

9 Finger crochet (page 31) a strap for your purse, and stitch an end to each side.

OTHER IDEAS

• Make the flap a different color, or make a striped purse.

• Make the purse in a stocking stitch (page 22).

• Sew on a Velcro closure instead of knitting a flap.

Striped mittens

These instructions make a pair of medium-sized kids' mittens. If you wish to make a large kids' pair, follow the bold number in each set of square brackets.

YOU WILL NEED

- 2 different-colored balls of knitting worsted weight yarn
- knitting needles, size 3.25 and 4.5 mm (U.S. 3 and 7)
- 2 stitch holders or large safety pins
- a ruler or measuring tape, scissors, a yarn needle

1 Make a slip knot about 1 m (1 yd.) from the end of one color of yarn. Cast 40 [**44**] stitches onto the 3.25 mm (U.S. 3) unmarked needle (step 2, page 22).

2 Knit one stitch and purl the next to the end of the row. Repeat, beginning each row with a knit stitch and ending with a purl stitch. You will be moving the yarn forward and back between each stitch to create single ribbing.

3 After four rows of single ribbing and with the stitches on the unmarked needle, change the color of yarn. Continue the ribbing for four rows of this color to make a stripe, then go back to the first color.

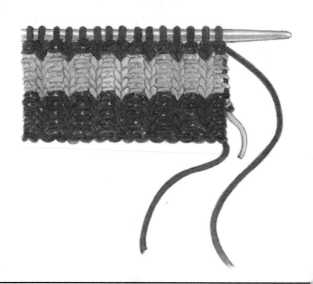

4 After four rows of the first color, make another four-row stripe with the second color, then go back to the first color for another four rows. All the stitches should be on the unmarked needle.

5 Use the marked 4.5 mm (U.S.7) needle to knit the next row. Use the unmarked large needle to purl the following row. Knit all the next row and purl the fourth.

6 Knit 18 [**20**] stitches, then increase (page 14) by 1 stitch into the 19th [**21st**] stitch. Knit 2 stitches. Increase by 1 in the next stitch, then knit the rest of the row. You should have 42 [**46**] stitches on the marked needle.

7 Purl the following row, knit the next row, and purl the row after that.

8 Knit 18 [**20**] stitches, then increase by 1 into the next stitch. Knit 4 stitches, then increase by 1 into the following stitch, and knit the rest of the row. You should have 44 [**48**] stitches on the marked needle.

9 Purl the next row. Change colors and make a stripe of stocking stitch (knit one row, purl the next) four rows wide. Do two more rows of stocking stitch in the first color. Cut the working yarn, leaving a 15 cm (6 in.) tail.

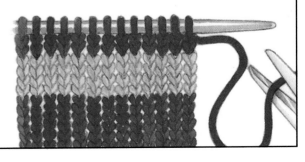

Instructions continue on the next page ☞

10 Slide the first 16 [**18**] stitches from the unmarked needle onto a stitch holder. Tie the first color of yarn (the same color you just cut off) to a line of yarn between stitch 16 [**18**] and 17 [**19**]. Knit the next 12 [**12**] stitches. Slip the next 16 [**18**] stitches onto the other stitch holder. Purl the 12 [**12**] remaining stitches.

12 Knit 2 stitches together along the next row so that you have 6 [**6**] stitches left. Purl the next row. Cut the working yarn, leaving a long tail. Thread the tail into the yarn needle and gather the remaining stitches off the knitting needle. Pull tight to close the top of the thumb, and turn it inside out. Make a few stitches on the same spot to hold it closed. Remove the yarn needle but don't cut the yarn.

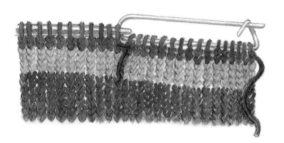

11 Knit 10 [**12**] rows of stocking stitch. Make a stripe in this thumb area, if you like. Finish with all the stitches on the unmarked needle.

13 With the good side of the knitting facing you, begin on the far left side to gather the stitches off the stitch holders onto the unmarked needle. Knot the working yarn back onto the right side. Begin with a row of knit stitches and continue across the thumb area as if there were no break in the row. Purl the next row and continue this stocking stitch until your mitten is about 19 [**22**] cm (7½ [**8½**] in.) long. Make a stripe or two in this area.

14 Begin to decrease. Knit 2 stitches together, knit 3 stitches, knit 2 together, knit 3 stitches to the end of the row, ending with knit 2 together [**ending with knit 4 stitches**]. Purl all 25 [**29**] stitches in the next row.

15 Knit 2 stitches together, knit 3 stitches, knit 2 together, knit 3 stitches to the end of the row, ending with knit 3 [**2**] stitches. Purl all 20 [**23**] stitches in the next row.

16 Knit 2 stitches together along the next row so that you have 10 [**12**] stitches left. Purl the next row.

17 Cut the working yarn, leaving a tail about 1 m (1 yd.) long. Thread the tail into the yarn needle and gather the remaining stitches off the needle.

18 Turn the mitten inside out and stitch together the top and side of the mitten. Line up the stripes as you sew. Make a few stitches on the same spot, knot the yarn end and trim it. Use the yarn at the top of the thumb to stitch the thumb closed, making sure there is no hole at the base.

19 Knot together, weave in and trim the other yarn ends inside the mitten. Turn it right side out and try it on. Roll up the cuff, if you like. Now knit the other mitten!

Pom-pom

Use pom-poms or tassels to jazz up your knitting. Use variegated yarn or different colors of yarn for a multicolored pom-pom.

1 Cut a piece of yarn about 75 cm (30 in.) long. Cut it in half and set it aside.

2 Hold your index and middle fingers apart as you wind yarn from the ball around them (use four fingers for a large pom-pom). Depending on the size of your fingers and the thickness of the yarn, you will need to wind between 50 and 100 times. Keep it loose enough so that it doesn't hurt, and keep a space between your fingers. Cut the yarn from the ball.

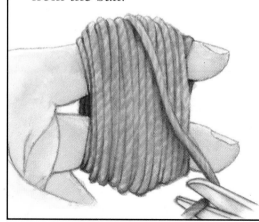

3 Take the two pieces of yarn from step 1 and push them between your fingers, on each side of the wound yarn. Tie them loosely with a double loop, as shown.

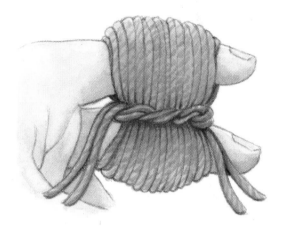

4 Gently slide the yarn off your fingers. Triple knot the yarn tightly in the center of the bundle of yarn. Cut open all the loops and trim your pom-pom, but don't trim the tying yarn ends. Hit the pom-pom against the edge of a table to fluff it. The more you trim your pom-pom, the smaller and thicker it will get.

Tassel

1 Wind yarn around a book or piece of cardboard about 10 cm (4 in.) wide. For thick yarn, wind it around about 20 times. For thin yarn, wind it around about 40 times. Cut the yarn from the ball.

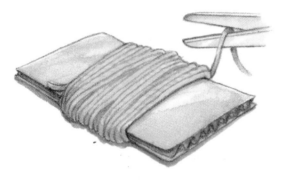

2 Cut a piece of yarn about 75 cm (30 in.) long and double it. Slip it under the yarn on one side of the book or cardboard, and knot it tightly at the top. Include the looped tying yarn end in the tassel and keep the other two ends free.

3 Slip the yarn off the book or cardboard. Cut another 75 cm (30 in.) piece of yarn and double it. Knot the yarn around the tassel about 2.5 cm (1 in.) down from the tied top. Let the tying yarn ends hang down with the other yarn in the tassel.

4 Cut all the looped ends of the tassel and trim them so they are even.

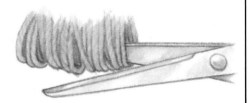

5 To attach the tassel to your knitted project, separate the ties at the top. Either poke them into your knitting and triple knot them, or thread them into a yarn needle and sew the tassel in place.

Boa

Many knitting patterns that you buy are given in abbreviations. Check the abbreviations in the box on this page, then follow these abbreviated instructions to knit a fun, feathery boa. The edges will curl nicely as it gets longer. Add a fringe, if you like.

With size 8 or 9 mm (U.S. 11 or 13) needles and a 50 g (1 ¾ oz.) ball of specialty feathery light yarn, cast on 16 sts. Work in St st until the boa is 1 m (1 yd.) long. Cast off and weave in yarn ends.

KNITTING ABBREVIATIONS

Here are some abbreviations for the steps and stitches used in this book:

beg	beginning
dec	decrease
ea	each
inc	increase
k	knit
k2tog	knit two together
mm	millimeters
p	purl
p2tog	purl two together
st(s)	stitch(es)
St st	stocking (stockinette) stitch
tog	together

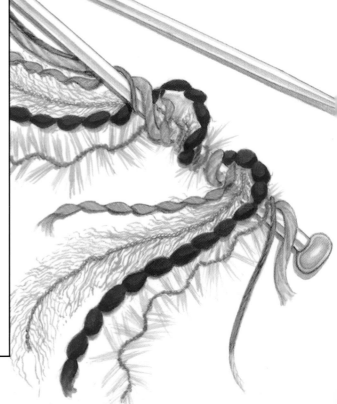